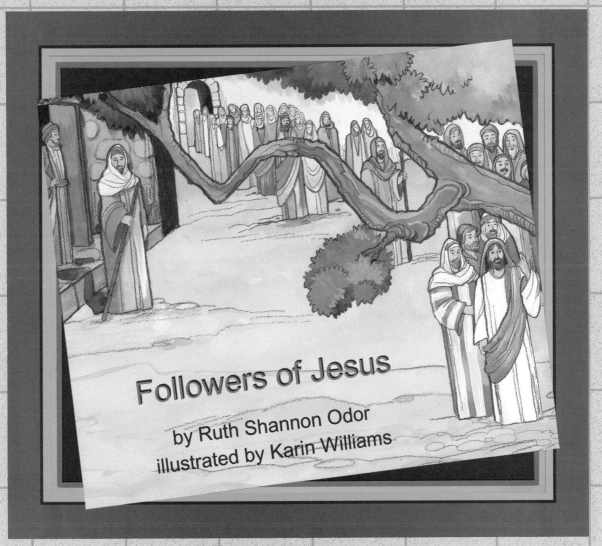

Followers of Jesus

by Ruth Shannon Odor

illustrated by Karin Williams

The Standard Publishing Company, Cincinnati, Ohio
A division of Standex International Corporation
© 1992 by The Standard Publishing Company
Printed in the United States of America
99 98 97 96 95 94 93 92   5 4 3 2 1
Library of Congress Catalog Card Number 91-67210
ISBN 0-87403-933-9

Jesus needed men to be His special helpers. One day Jesus walked by the Sea of Galilee. He saw two brothers. They were fishing.

Do you know who they were?

TURN THE PAGE ▶▶▶

AND SEE

Peter and Andrew were the fishermen.
Jesus said to them, "Follow me."
And they did.
They left their boats and nets.
Peter and Andrew became followers
of Jesus.

As Jesus walked on, He saw two more brothers.
They were in a boat with their father.
They were repairing their fishing nets.
Do you know who they were?

TURN THE PAGE ▶▶▶▶

AND SEE

The two brothers were James and John.
Jesus said to them, "Follow me."
And they did.
They left their father and their boat.
James and John became followers of Jesus.

O ne day Jesus saw a man sitting at a table.
He was collecting money for taxes.
The man was a tax collector.
Do you know who he was?

TURN THE PAGE ▶▶▶

AND SEE

The man's name was Matthew.
Jesus said to him, "Follow me."
And he did.
He left his work of collecting taxes.
Matthew became a follower of Jesus.

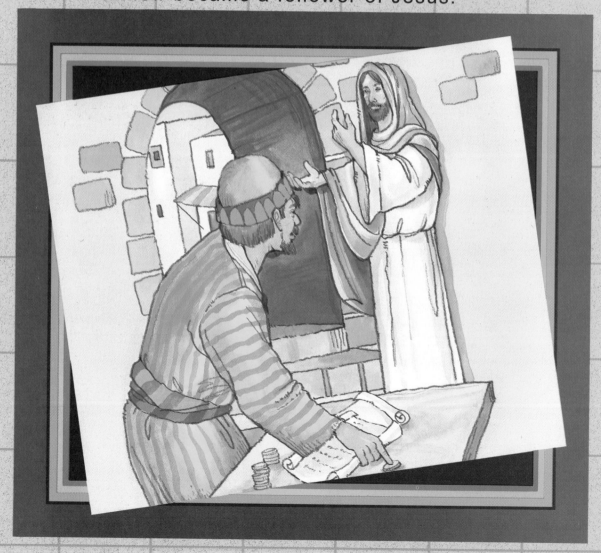

Another day Jesus found a man and said to
    him, "Follow me."
The man wanted to be a follower of Jesus.
He hurried to his friend Nathanael.
He told Nathanael about Jesus.
Do you know who the man was?

TURN THE PAGE

AND SEE

The man was Philip.
Philip took his friend Nathanael to Jesus.
Both Philip and Nathanael became followers
  of Jesus.

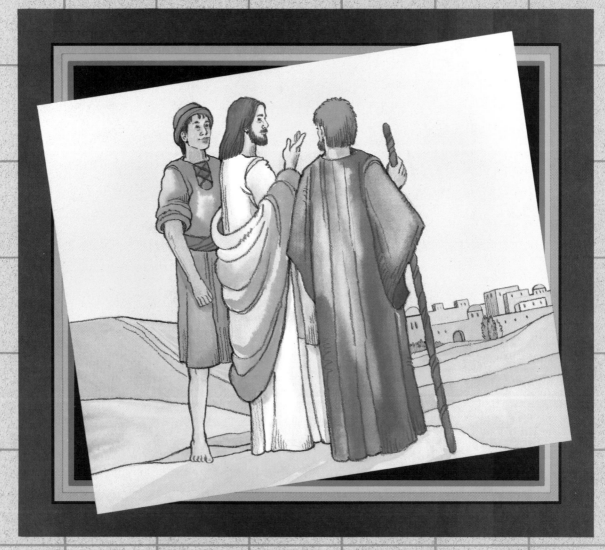

Now Peter and Andrew, James and John,
Matthew, Philip, and Nathanael
all followed Jesus.
Jesus asked five other men to be His special
followers or helpers.
How many men did this make?

TURN THE PAGE

AND SEE

There were 12 special followers, or helpers, of Jesus.
They were called apostles.

They listened to Jesus teach.
They worked for Jesus.
The twelve apostles followed Jesus.

A man lived in the city of Jericho.
The man was a dishonest tax collector.
He wanted to see Jesus, but he was very
  short.
He could not see Jesus because of the crowd.

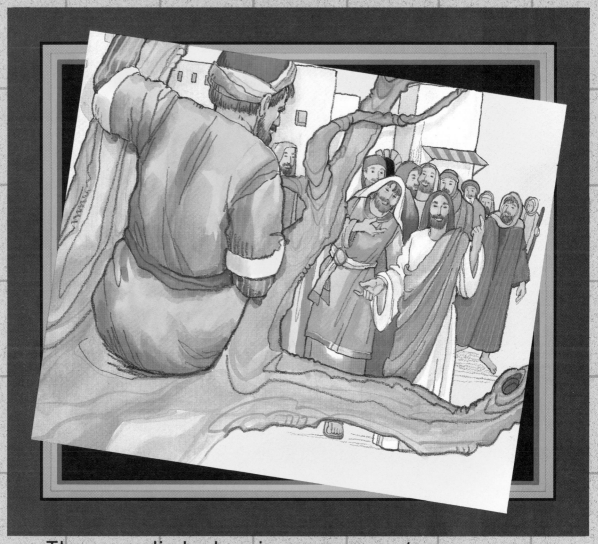

The man climbed up in a sycamore tree.
Then he could see Jesus.
Do you know the short man's name?

TURN THE PAGE ▶▶▶

AND SEE

The short man's name was Zacchaeus.
Jesus went to Zacchaeus' home for dinner.
Jesus talked with Zacchaeus.
Zacchaeus decided to change. He became a
   good and honest man.
Zacchaeus became a follower of Jesus.

Once a woman was very sick.
Then she met Jesus one day.
Jesus made the woman well.
How thankful she was to Jesus.
Do you know who the woman was?

TURN THE PAGE ▶▶▶

AND SEE

The woman's name was Mary Magdalene.
She was sad when she saw Jesus die on the cross.
She was sad as she came to His tomb early the
    next morning.
But she was happy when Jesus spoke to her!
She was glad that Jesus was alive!
Mary Magdalene was a follower of Jesus.

Jesus had returned to Heaven to live with God.
His followers were busy working for Him.
But there was a man who did not think that
    Jesus was God's Son.
On a trip to Damascus, Jesus spoke to him.
Then the man knew that he had been wrong.
Do you know who the man was?

TURN THE PAGE ▶▶▶

AND SEE

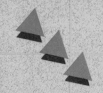

The man was Saul. Later he was called Paul.
Saul became a Christian.
He traveled to many lands and preached and
    taught about Jesus.
Paul spent the rest of his life working for
    Jesus.
Paul was truly a follower of Jesus.

A man from Cyprus lived in Jerusalem.
He sold part of his land and gave the money to
   the church.
Later he was a friend to Saul.
He took Saul to the church leaders. He told them
   that now Saul believed Jesus is God's Son.
Do you know who the man was?

TURN THE PAGE

AND SEE

The man was Barnabas.
Barnabas traveled with Paul.
They went to many different towns.
They preached and taught about Jesus.
Barnabas was a follower of Jesus.

One day a boy heard Paul preach.
The boy's mother and grandmother had taught
   him about God.
But they did not know about Jesus, God's Son.
After the boy heard Paul preach, he became a
   Christian.
Do you know the boy's name?

TURN THE PAGE

AND SEE

The boy's name was Timothy.
One day Paul asked Timothy to go with him
 and work for Jesus.
Timothy was glad to go with Paul.
Timothy was a follower of Jesus.

Paul was in the city of Corinth.
He met a man and wife who sewed tents and
   sold them.
That was the kind of work Paul did, too.
Paul stayed in their home, and all three
   worked at making tents.
Do you know who the man and woman were?

TURN THE PAGE

AND SEE

The man was Aquila and his wife was Priscilla.
They became Paul's helpers.
They even left home and traveled far away
    to tell people about Jesus.
Aquila and Priscilla were followers of Jesus.

Jesus needs followers today.
He needs men and women, boys and girls,
    to work for Him.
Who will be a follower of Jesus?

TURN THE PAGE ▶▶▶

AND SEE

Paste your picture here.

We can be followers of Jesus.
We can love Him best of all.
We can obey Him.
We can work for Him.

_____will follow Jesus.
(Write your name here.)